NEPAL TREK
On Top of the World

Sharlene G. Coombs

KNOWLEDGE
BOOKS AND SOFTWARE

2

Teacher Notes:

This story recounts a trek to Mera Peak in the Himalayan Mountain region of Nepal. It explores the beauty and culture of this country and the kindness and resilience of its people, as well as the challenges of high altitude, extreme cold and physical exhaustion.

Discussion activities for consideration:

1. Discuss what the author would have had to do to prepare for this trek.

2. Talk about the pros and cons of this kind of tourism for Nepal.

3. Share a goal that you would like to achieve and how you would plan for it.

4. What problems or issues would you need to address along the way?

Difficult words to be introduced and practised before reading this book:

Himalayas, altitude, Buddhist, monastery, preparation, Mera La, Kathmandu, Sir Edmund Hillary, New Zealand, Mt Everest, Tenzing Norgay, challenging, rock-climbing, experience, crazier, drop-offs, oncoming, dangerous, exhausted, Sherpas, awesome, haven, Nepalese, original, acclimatise, recover, Namaste, Buddhists, religion, seriously, icicles, evacuated, oxygen, resilient, generations, Tibetan, zig-zagged, Lama, kata, protection, exposed, crampons, self-arrest, ice-axes, glacier, igloos, routine, frostbite, avalanche, cancelled, mountaineering, Lukla, celebrated, military, Afghanistan.

Contents

1. Off to the Himalayas!

2. Altitude Training and Culture

3. Buddhist Monastery Blessing

4. Summit Preparation

5. Mera La – the Pass

6. Back to Kathmandu

1. Off to the Himalayas!

Ever since I was a kid, I'd dreamed of visiting the Himalayas. I'd read stories about Sir Edmund Hillary, the famous New Zealand climber. He was the first to climb Mt Everest with Sherpa Tenzing Norgay.

In my teens, I got into hiking in Tassie. I hiked most of the treks there. But I wanted something more challenging. You can't get more challenging than the Himalayas! So, I did some research and found Mera Peak. At 6476m, Mera Peak is the highest trekking peak in the world. This means that you don't need rock-climbing experience to climb it. However, you do need to be very fit. The altitude is seriously high. I was hooked! So, I saved and trained!

Six months later, I arrived in Kathmandu. I met my group for a pre-trek talk. Then we piled into a crazy bus and drove 8 long hours to the start of our trek.

The only thing crazier than the bus were the drivers! The roads were narrow and winding with sheer drop-offs. Those guys didn't slow down around the corners. They just held their hand on the horn to let the oncoming cars know they were coming. Looking back, I think it might have been the most dangerous part of our trip!

We arrived at Jiri later that day. We were tired and happy to be alive! After setting up camp, we met our porters and sherpas. These guys are legends. The porters carried the heavy gear each day. The sherpas were our guides and cooks.

Sherpas are the local Nepali people. They come from many different mountain villages. Helping climbers is the major job in the area. They carry the food, equipment and get the trail ready. When a climber gets lost, they go out in all weather to find them. They are tough and fit but still find it hard in the high mountains. Many of them die in the mountains from accidents during climbing trips. It's a dangerous job but it pays very well.

The cooks made an awesome meal that night in the mess tent. This place was to become a haven for us at the end of each long day. We made new friends and shared amazing Nepalese meals there.

The next morning, we started our climb along the original trekking route to Everest. I kept thinking about all the famous climbers that had trod this path. Now I was doing it too! We passed lots of little villages along the way. Many were poor and didn't have much, but they were all so happy and smiling.

We trekked into a beautiful river valley that afternoon. We set up camp and chilled out by the river. Day 1 of 22 was pretty easy but we all knew it was about to get a whole lot harder!

2. Altitude Training and Culture

The next few days of our trek were all about getting used to the altitude. When you reach a certain altitude, it can affect your body in different ways. Around 3000m, you can sometimes feel sick and get headaches. It affects some people differently. The best way to avoid altitude sickness is to acclimatise to it. To do this, you should always sleep lower than your highest altitude for the day. This gives your body a chance to recover overnight before going higher again.

The next day, we found ourselves climbing through some huge forests. The branches were covered in moss and there was mist everywhere. We were in the clouds! It felt like we were in a 'Lord of the Rings' movie.

The foothills were scattered with lots of villages along the way. The kids would come out to say "Namaste" and wish us good luck. I had packed some pencils and stickers to give to them. They thought that was cool!

Most of the Nepalese people are Buddhists. They take their religion very seriously. Along the route, we saw several prayer walls with prayer wheels. As they walk past these walls, they spin the prayer wheels. Spinning the wheel is like saying a prayer. It's designed to bring good luck.

Prayer flags were also scattered all along the way. Prayers are written on each flag. The wind moves across them to scatter kindness and good feelings to everyone. How clever is that!

We woke to freezing weather on Day 8. The clouds had come in and light snow was falling. Our highest and longest climb so far was ahead of us.

We climbed around the side of a huge mountain with a steep drop-off. We had to be so careful. Icicles were hanging off rock ledges everywhere. We had now reached over 4000m. Some of us had headaches but nothing too serious.

We found out later that someone from another group was evacuated. He started turning blue from lack of oxygen. The guides put him in a portable pressure bag to make it feel like he was at a lower altitude. However, when he came out, he got worse. They were very worried and had the guy taken out in a chopper.

3. Buddhist Monastery Blessing!

After our big climb, we spent the next few days trekking through sherpa villages. Crops were growing and yaks were grazing. Some locals were carrying big bundles of firewood on their backs. Even the women and children did their fair share of the carrying. These people were very strong and resilient. They had lived off the land for many generations. The mountains were their life!

A highlight of the trip for many of us was a visit to a traditional Tibetan Buddhist Monastery. We came across monks doing daily chores and saying their prayers. The monastery was built into the side of a mountain. Prayer flags zig-zagged up the mountain behind it. It felt very peaceful.

We were lucky to be blessed by the Lama, the head of the monastery. Each of us gave him a kata, a white scarf. This is tradition. He then gave this back to each of us. The meaning of this was: the more you give, the more you receive. He also gave each of us a red string to tie around our necks. It's a protection and blessing cord to help keep you safe. The Lama invited us to have Tibetan tea with him. We'd been told it's bad manners not to drink it. It was made of yak butter and lots of salt. Let's just say, Tibetan tea is not really my thing!

We spent the next 4 days climbing along high ridges. We were now above the treeline at over 4500m. It was cold and windy and very exposed.

4. Summit Preparation

Snow arrived on day 17. It was falling steadily now and getting colder by the minute. A few of us were sick. This made it even harder, but we pushed on. You didn't have a choice, so we dug deep like the locals did! They inspired us.

The next day was a gear sorting day. The guide helped us to attach crampons to our boots to give us grip when walking on ice. He also showed us how to self-arrest with our ice-axes, just in case we fell.

We then explored an amazing glacier and lake nearby. A year later, part of this glacier broke off and smashed into the lake. It caused massive flooding in some of the villages.

Day 19 was Base Camp Day! We climbed steadily out of the valley and up through snow-covered rocks. This area had once been a glacier. It had carved out the valley and dropped lots of massive rocks along the way. We were now over 4700m high. Many of us were feeling short of breath due to the lack of oxygen.

We finally arrived at Base Camp and set up. It started snowing about 8pm and stopped around 4am the next morning. In 8 hours, more than a metre of snow fell. The campsite looked like a heap of little igloos popping up out of the earth. The sherpas even had to dig us out of our tents! This was pretty cool but the best thing about the next morning was the sun shining.

5. Mera La – the Pass

The porters didn't climb any further than Base Camp for safety reasons. This meant that we had to carry our own gear up to the summit. We packed only what we really needed and headed off.

Our climb up from Base Camp to the pass at Mera La was slow and exhausting. The snow that had fallen overnight was even deeper further up. One of the guides had gone ahead to clear a path, but it was still very hard going. The air was so much thinner and we were struggling to catch our breath. We got into a routine of 10 steps, then a breather. It was mind over matter. You just had to keep going.

We put one foot in front of the other and finally made it to the pass late in the afternoon. It had taken us the whole day to climb just 700m. Normally it is easy to set up a tent, but it is very hard at 5400m. You even had to take a break when tying your shoelaces!

We had to be very careful of frostbite. Frostbite happens when your skin is exposed to the extreme cold. The layers of your skin can start to freeze. It normally affects areas like your fingers and toes. The temperature dropped to -20 degrees Celsius that night. Frostbite can start in a minute.

Without the sherpas and porters, we only had the basics. Dinner was some fruit and nuts and chocolate. We ate this slowly. Even though we had been climbing hard all day, some of us had lost our appetite. This is all part of altitude sickness. Eating can make you feel sick, but you still have to eat to keep up your energy levels.

We scrambled into our tents early to try and get some rest. All that was between us and the freezing snow was our sleeping bag and the thin tent floor. We all slept three to a tent that night. None of us got much sleep!

After a rough night's sleep, we woke early. It was summit day! It was still dark but the sky was clear. Clouds can sometimes trap warm air in and make it feel warmer. However, there were no clouds about that morning. This made it even colder. We layered up to make sure we had no exposed skin. One of our group had a touch of frostbite on the tips of his fingers. His shoelaces had frozen in his boots the night before. While trying to undo them, his fingers had been exposed to the freezing air for too long. Others had been suffering from the extremely high altitude overnight. Some had very bad headaches but were keen to push on.

The guides were talking quietly between themselves. They looked concerned. They called a meeting with us.

There had been news of avalanche danger in the area. The heavy snow that had fallen two nights ago was still soft and unstable. The weather had warmed up and the snow hadn't set to ice yet.

The guides did an avalanche test to make sure. Sure enough, the top layer of snow slid straight off. They had to cancel the summit attempt because it was just too dangerous. This was as far as we'd be going. We were all so gutted, but we understood the need for safety first.

6. Back to Kathmandu

With the summit attempt cancelled, we packed up our tents and slowly made our way back down to Base Camp. We had come so close! But at least we were alive to tell the tale. Too many climbers had taken the risk and paid the price with their lives in the past.

Sometimes, at this kind of altitude, your thinking and judgement can be affected. It can make you do things that you wouldn't normally do. Our guides were thinking of our safety first and foremost. Some had taken the news harder than others and felt they had failed. This wasn't the case. We'd taken the smart option and were still here to talk about it. No one can control Mother Nature!

The climb down was easier and the weather was still fine. We had views of huge peaks all around us, including a glimpse of Mt Everest!

As the weather warmed up during the day, we had to be careful. The Sun was melting the snow quite quickly. This was causing some crevasses to open up. Snow bridges had once covered these and made it safe to walk over. Crevasses are like huge cracks in the ice which can be very deep. Climbers have lost their lives falling into crevasses before. We looked for signs of cracks in the ice and made it back to Base Camp.

Over the next few days, we started our descent back down the mountains. The bad weather came in again and the snow turned to heavy rain and sleet.

The weather had also turned nasty on the mountain peaks. On the way down, we heard that some climbers were rescued off a mountain not far from Mera Peak. They had been caught in a small avalanche and one of the climbers had broken his leg. They had also lost some of their supplies and were low on food. Our decision to turn back proved to be a good one!

After 22 days of trekking and climbing, we finally arrived at our destination, Lukla. This town makes a living out of transporting climbers in and out of the Himalayas.

It has one of the craziest airstrips I've ever seen! It's very short and on an angle. It also drops straight off a cliff! There are a few plane wrecks along the edge of it. I was really glad we were flying out in a helicopter!

We couldn't quite believe that it was finished! We all celebrated that night. The next day, we loaded our gear into the waiting chopper. It was an old army chopper with bullet holes.

The chopper was just a shell inside with bench seats on both sides. Just before we took off, the pilot came round with cotton wool for our ears. This was to protect our ears from the noise of the chopper. It was deafening!

We crossed our fingers and made it safely back to Kathmandu, Nepal's capital. We had a couple of days to explore this amazing city before our flight back home. There are really cool temples and buildings and shops!

As we flew out of Nepal, we had great views of the Himalayan mountain range. It's the biggest mountain range in the world and attracts climbers from around the world. It crosses China, Pakistan, India, Tibet, Nepal and Bhutan. Looking at these huge, jagged peaks poking out of the clouds was an awesome sight!

This trip of a lifetime really had everything. Nature, climbing, hard work, culture, teamwork, friendship and pure adventure. I'll cherish this memory forever.

Word Bank

Himalayas	dangerous	generations
altitude	exhausted	Tibetan
Buddhist	Sherpas	zig-zagged
Monastery	awesome	Lama
preparation	haven	kata
Mera La	Nepalese	protection
Kathmandu	original	exposed
Sir Edmund Hillary	acclimatise	crampons
	recover	self-arrest
New Zealand	Namaste	ice-axes
Mt Everest	Buddhists	glacier
Tenzing Norgay	religion	igloos
challenging	seriously	routine
rock-climbing	icicles	frostbite
experience	evacuated	avalanche
crazier	oxygen	cancelled
drop-offs	resilient	mountaineering
oncoming		